# The Dance Floor Tilts

# The Dance Floor Tilts

Susan Alexander

Dear Ray —
Happy birthday & happy
reading! Susan XO

17 December, 2017

*thistledown press*

Thistledown Press Ltd.
410 2nd Avenue North
Saskatoon, Saskatchewan, S7K 2C3
www.thistledownpress.com

Library and Archives Canada Cataloguing in Publication

Alexander, Susan Thelma, author
The dance floor tilts / Susan Alexander.
Poems.
ISBN 978-1-77187-152-5 (softcover)
I. Title.
PS8601.L348D36 2017     C811'.6     .C2017-905324-8

Cover: *Highway Kiss*, 1999 by Andrew Valko
Cover and book design by Jackie Forrie
Printed and bound in Canada

Thistledown Press gratefully acknowledges the financial assistance of the Canada
Council for the Arts, the Saskatchewan Arts Board, and the Government of
Canada for its publishing program.

## ACKNOWLEDGEMENTS

I wish to thank the following journals, chapbook and anthology where several of these poems first appeared: *Contemporary Verse 2, Grain Magazine, Arc Poetry Magazine, The Antigonish Review, Prism International, Crux, Room, Vanishing into the Leaves* and *This Island We Celebrate.*

Deepest thanks to my friend and mentor, Lorna Crozier, for her exuberant love of poetry, her inspired teaching and generous support of my work. Thank you to poetry friends and teachers — to David Pimm, Laura Apol, Barbara Pelman, Pamela Porter, Arleen Pare, Jude Neale, Wendy Morton, Richard Osler, to Rena Upitis and the Wintergreen Poets, to Liz McNally and the Honeymoon Bay Poets and to Patrick Lane.

Thank you to Thistledown Press, and especially Seán Virgo for his invaluable guidance with the manuscript. Also to Winnipeg artist Andrew Valko for the cover, *Highway Kiss.*

Many thanks to family and friends for their encouragement and to my husband, Ross McDonald, without whom I would still be hiding my poems in a closet instead of printing them on the pages of this book.

# CONTENTS

## What Are You Made Of?

## Her Own Late Self

## HOW THE LIGHT CHANGES

## MINISTERS OF GRACE

*for Thelma and Jim*

# WHAT ARE YOU MADE OF?

# BEDTIME STORY

In the upstairs room where we three
sisters slept, rosebuds covered walls,
coverlets. Even the beds wore frilled skirts.

Gone early, home late, he was more shadow
than father, but suddenly, there.
Heavy and huge at the end of the bed
his furred hands, a smack of tobacco,
rye and gasoline. Engine grease
etched lines across pink palms.
He scoured us with whiskers.

And then his question:
*How much do you love me?*
Always the same trick. My sisters held
out arms willing and wide while I
tucked baby elbows tight against sides,
hands a chest-width apart.
I watched my sisters squeal and shriek,
until I risked all, opened my wings
to show him how much.

His tickling fingers hooked too hard,
too deep. A reflex laugh masked
my howl, betrayed my tears.
Love left me limp.

I wore our play like an ache, raw
as a stone in a shoe. I had my question
too. Scared to ask. I feared an answer
I thought I knew. *How much? How much?*

SPY

You wake after midnight
to catch her staring
through the window.

She tries to hide
behind the cottonwood,
pulls clouds
across her wide face.

You watch her
from under Grammy's quilt,
its knotted squares
of work shirts and trust.

Her whisper silvers the leaves:
*What are you made of?*

# THE AVALON

It was a fast food joint on Highway 3
where it turned into Main Street.
Picnic tables in the breezeway, Creedence
screaming up around the bend on the jukebox.
No drive-thru windows like today.
People had to park, get out of their cars.

My father was boss, shape-shifted
from grease monkey in his own garage
to short order cook.  Short temper cook
more like it. Hotter than burgers sizzling
on the grill. Hotter than chips in the deep fat fryer.
Him and his shout and his bottomless rum
and coke just inside the cooler door.

Scariest thing for me was making
chicken dinners when he was crazy
busy and the grill was packed. I'd crank
up the flames under the pressure cooker
in the back, drop thighs, legs, breasts,
wings, into popping oil then twist
the metal top on tight as I could.

Timing was critical and I was racing
up front with customers at windows,
making change with fingers burnt
from bagging burgers. Milkshakes
whizzed on metal sticks while I erected
dazzling ziggurats of soft ice cream cones.

All the time at the back the pressure
built. Always I expected the explosion.
My father's holler. Flying metal, boiling oil.
Fast food shrapnel. Casualties.

When the cooker's valves got flipped up,
they screamed like murder, smeared the air
with steam and grease. I served up impossible
crispy gold in a cardboard container.

For years I wore burn scars
on the soft insides of forearms.
They are faded, almost gone.
So is my father.
Nowadays summer never gets that hot.

# CUCKOO

Just before the hour, it would gently groan.
A tiny couple popped out and circled
to the Bavarian tune. Next the cuckoo.

Three long bronze pinecones
lolled against the wall like drunks
when the clock wound down. Then whined,
zippered into place.

It was after three when I got caught.
I slammed my bedroom door so hard
the clock arced from the kitchen wall.
It hung in the air,
then shattered at my father's feet.

He gathered up the pieces and spread them
on his bench. For weeks, he fiddled with
broken parts if he had the time.
When I snuck past the shed, I'd hear him
swearing under his breath.

My father was no patient watchmaker. Still,
he got the cuckoo bowing the hours again.
But the music stopped.
The little man and woman never danced again.

# FORAGING

He shuts the backdoor
on the argument,
squats beside the garden,
slides open a pack of Players.
Smoke curls
over his upper lip,
vanishes into nostrils.
He counts the rows.

Wasp-hollowed pears
lie among the last beans.
Arugula chokes the lettuce.
He considers this,
bites the tip of a leaf.
His mouth fills
with bitterness.

# NABEITA

My grandmother crochets, cupped in the orange chair
in the kitchen corner. It's Scandinavian like her.
A thousand years ago, she was lured
from the island farm on Frøya, sent
a ship's ticket and the promise of luxury.
She'd keep house in her brother's imagined mansion.
Instead Ivor tugged her up Jervis Inlet,
cook for the logging camp.

Half grown, I half listen, half watch TV as she
talks. Then she hooks me with her child-round cheeks,
her eyes washed silk behind upturned glasses.
*He hoodwinked me. My own brother.*

In time, Ivor built his big house in Shaughnessy,
filled it with wife, children and fine furniture.
His homesick sister married and mothered ten
plus her husband who lost more than a hand to a peat cutter.
Widowed, she drifts from home to home.
Ours now. Her houseshift emits a newborn scent.
Talcum powder. Her hair gleams white in its net
as she bends, smoothing the web of lace against her lap.

# THE RACK

That summer job
at Mike's drugstore
in Osoyoos meant
windowless
coffeebreaks amid
returned merchandise
and damaged goods.
While I chewed through
cheap boxes of leprous
chocolates and emptied
indifferent sweets
from burst bags,
I'd study the shiny girls,
thin as paper,
who lounged
on sailboats
and south sea atolls.

> My polyester blue uniform tightened.
> My belly and thighs swelled like rising dough.

My favourite
had a gap between
her front teeth
like me. I knew all
their glossy
names, ages,
heights, weights.
Silent between slender
magazine sheets, they
witnessed my decline.
Some were startled
by the cellophane

crunch. Others
were cryptic
as the last toffee
cleared the bag
in the airless staffroom.

A local boy at the dance, slurred,
*Didn't you used to be beautiful?*

The covers came off
at the end of the month
when the latest issues
hit the rack. I took
the ditched ones
home with me
into our detached
garage. They watched
me open the deep
freeze with its
buckets and tins
of ice cream
and Mum's
oatmeal-coconut
cookies, waferthin,
especially crisp
when frozen.

Each bite cut flesh like some girls do.
Instead of sleeves, I hid in subcutaneous layers.

Airbrushed beauties
rustled their pages,
arching towards
each other, all
hollow cheeks,
Chicklet smiles.

# LISTENING TO CHARLIE PARKER

saxophonesexophonesexonthephonephoneforsex
hands grip thick thighs slip saliva over under ride it
sound so wide it slides big gold dick slick with music
tears and tongue saxon slut flaxen strumpet

wet as malt whiskey cut crystal no ice
soft as chinchilla coat take it off taken from behind
press there and therelessly careless mind elsewhere
in the air warm washed fall in deep down

sunset mouth slack fingers search something smooth
tabletop glass lips earlobe knead and pull
knead and press tuck cup cheek caress a long tress

sound that turns riffs round aural ruffies downed
with one big shisha toke please squeeze unzip slip
back hiked against smooth grained wood boned
chord bound limbic kick jazz walk eyes open slow

## SORTING CHERRIES

We sat in lines on either side
of the belt's endless loop. Across from me,
a woman in her fifties, black hair dull with dye,
flanked by cronies. She listed infirmities
as numerous as the cherries rolling by.
Her hands darted, deft as a lacemaker,
picked out the split and the bruised.

Beside me, the tough girls I drank
with in high school. The ones who still smoked,
who had sex in the back of Camaros
belonging to boyfriends who worked
at the mill. Girls who weren't headed
to university when summer was over.

After eight days, the whistle blew for break
and the belt stopped. I fell off my stool.
Mesmerized. The foreman moved me
up the chain. Alone. I pushed boxes of Bings
around a corner. When that crop was done,
we all got laid off until the next call came.
I never went back.

Some nights before sleep, I see them glide by,
a stream of profligate hearts.

## BLUE

*after "Sounding the Name" by Robert Kroetsch*

In this poem, I don't go to university.
My parents don't look up from mounds
of motel laundry and crush my plan
for Europe on five dollars a day.

I don't rent an attic room in a house
shared by strangers. I don't take
the word of a poli-sci major
that my first year doesn't matter while we
hot-knife hashish in the kitchen before class.

In this poem, I don't skip second semester
to drink beer, proof the student rag, ache
for its editor, fail my Latin exam. I don't down
doughnuts, date squares, frozen Sara Lee.
My thighs don't play accordion when I walk
in my cords. Before the worn fabric tears.

No. In this poem my parents put up the No Vacancy
sign and drive me five hours to the airport.

On Milos, I wash the day's salt from my skin,
slide silver on my arms and walk in the breeze
to the hilltop taverna. I set out green olives
in a blue dish. Later, in a fisherman's bed,
I will spoon, I will sleep.

## FULL FATHOM FIVE

        Creosote-soaked
summer morning by the pilings where you
used to mooch for salmon. White-haired
anemones wave underwater.
Your children kneel with you for the first
and last time, knees grind on the swim grid.
We cradle the hand-turned urn and watch
ashes hematite flash in the thick green deep.
Glints like lures.

        Words empty.
Solemnity dries into silence, into thirst.
We get drunk, splash in with shrieks.
Our flesh-enrobed bones move among
your scattered flakes, swim through
this underwater star cloud. Your wife dives
headlong into your depths, tastes you again,
salt and wet on her tongue. You lick her
everywhere, stroke her hair. Hold her,
hold all of us again.

        Bone chips like crushed
mussels. You were a shell at the end, withered
limbs splayed on the couch, only your belly soft,
prednisone swollen. How you loved a trim torso.
How you used to turn sideways to show us, show off.
We two were tongue-tied at the end,
while my fingers waved goodbye, feathered
your hair, fluttered over chalky hollows
of cheek and socket.

Before the fire chamber,
your wax manikin lay boxed, an unlit candle.
Only the wick, your hair unchanged, already
dead for months. It pulled us into flood tides,
hands lost in a white sea.

# THE MILKMAN

Call it fanciful. Call it environmental, but I buy my milk in
bottles. Cow's milk. The kind that clots in the bottle's neck,
though not the way it used to way back when before I was
born. Back then Dad drove a horse and cart from FraSea
Farms on Sea Island across the river on the Marpole swing
bridge and down Vancouver avenues. Replaced empty
with full. Glass clink and horse's breath, dawn mists and
downpours.

He was handsome, a favourite with the Kerrisdale matrons.
Around Christmas he came home from his route with tawny
bottles — rum, rye and scotch — tucked in beside the empties
for some holiday cheer. Sometimes along the route a door
would open and he'd be pulled inside for coffee and cake, a
casual chat. One morning he set down the usual order on a
stoop when a sudden husband loomed and snatched the cap
off his head. The newborn wailing in the man's arms was a
tiny carrot top, and that day Dad sure was lucky he wasn't a
redhead.

In time, truck replaced horse, bottles became cartons, opaque.
The dairy got paved for runways. Dad changed too. He turned
to mechanics and auto parts, got his own station with hoists
and gas pumps. Glass holds visions I never saw. Call it senti-
mental or call it what you will…

## CANNED PEACHES

At the table, my mother's hands,
unusually still, cradle her cup.
She stares at nothing, framed by teak
cabinets my father hung on the fake
brick wall. Under her, the avocado lino
he installed. Her jack of all trades.
Master of none, he would add if here.
We are alone. He's in a hospital bed.
She asks me if she ruined his life.

He should've been an engineer,
she says. He had the brains.
The babies, seven to feed, somehow
her fault. He could've done better,
she says. Last born, I sit and listen
to words she will never repeat.

Evening light crowds in the open
storeroom door. It climbs jars
of cherries, pears, mustard pickles,
raspberry jam stacked between studs
of a wall he never finished.
They glow like a chapel window.
In the kitchen, I twist the ring,
break the seal, spoon peaches
into bowls, tip in a syrup so sweet
it makes my teeth ache.

# GENESIS

She taught me colours back when I was stuck
between raw bones and sudden curves.

*Look how beautiful.*

She pointed to the dead outside the car window,
the orchards' naked ranks, stony mountains.

I slumped in the seat. She pulled over, pulled me
out onto the road's gray shoulder.

Paint-smudged hands danced shapes across
a sepia world —

| willow | *cadmium* |
| dogwood | *vermillion* |
| winter grass | *burnt umber, ochre, sienna* |

Flame wavered on the sky's edge,
straked the valley.

The first day.

## HOME FROM ROME

Just yesterday, all that light. Fountains like molten gold
at every corner. Such riches for everyone. Even the beggars.

The girl who sat outside the Pantheon on her skateboard,
twisted feet on display. Her skin glowed, golden.
Even the man with stubs where arms and legs should be. Gold.

Here morning moves in dimly, all remains grey
even as May comes to a close. The lilac's fat leaves suck all light
from the sky. Blooms nod, homely as sock horses.

# MONET'S BRIDGE

Spring, and I coax my mother to Paris
for her very first time. She's sixty-six,
just sold the motel. I whizz her
through rooms of Impressionists.

In the Jeu de Paume, she gazes
at the Japanese bridge, then skips over it
to the Orangerie where she wades
to her knees through lilies

along curved walls. At the Opera
she floats to the dome,
whirls with Chagall's tutu'd dancers,
waltzes to Verdi's *Masked Ball*.

Back home she keeps her small-town
feet on the ground with ankle weights.
She opens her paint box
and goes to work for decades.

The walls fill with flowers.

## MAKER

Her hands are vises.
They seem too powerful for her slight frame.
Between them red clay spins.

She curves forward,
elbows at right angles,
feet planted wide.

A bowl rises out of the mud.
Discarded piles multiply
on the basement floor beside her
like rock towers of Cappadocia.

*Can I come with you, mother,*
*to the place where you go*
*at your wheel, alone?*
*I have kicked the ground at Konya,*
*unearthed potsherds and handles,*
*peered at your cups behind*
*the glass in foreign museums.*
*Mother, your hands are ancient.*

She stops her wheel. Grabbing a wire,
she garrotes the bowl off its base,
then stretches out her marled fingers
beside mine, so clean so white.

# THE PYSCHIATRIC NURSE

Some stories haunt me after she dies. Like who she was before her seven kids. The mental hospital up the valley where she'd trained and lived after high school. One time I sat beside her while she mended our clothes and she took me on rounds down antiseptic halls.

Back then they zapped the patients. Electroshock therapy. No antipsychotics. Back then she wore keys that clanged on a ring at her waist and every door was locked. She opened one once and got slugged. Only once. Disturbed was the word they used for that ward. "She didn't see *me*," Mum said. "She saw a monster." There was Mildred who was harmless. She banged her shoe and stamped her foot shouting *murder, murder* all day long. Her right side grew bigger than her left from all that beating. Ruth was a beauty who dolled herself up, leaned against the window's bars and whistled at my dad whenever he came to call. Before he married Mum. Before Ruth's lobotomy.

Mum used to say that we all have our crazy ways. When I was small, she listened to dizzy fears — the toilet witch, the one who hid inside the flush. At fourteen, I tripped out on LSD. She didn't get mad, she wanted to know about hallucinations. I saw it once, the institution. Its doors had opened then closed long before; its patients spilled into skid row with fistfuls of pills. Shattered panes gaped in rows like comic book drawings; broken teeth, sockets in a dry skull.

HER OWN LATE SELF

## ECHO 1, SHE IS NOT SHE

until he breathes softly,
rolls over and pushes
away the comforter. Before that,

nothing.
No walls or bed.
In the silence

she listens
for evidence
that she exists: rain
splatter against the pane,
scrape of cedar,
tide-wash through beach pebbles.

The waves cannot find her.
The wind has lost
her name.

Each morning when he wakes,
he reels her back.

## ECHO 2, PHASE

The old cliché — he was earth
to her moon. She waxed
and waned with his disposition.
Always she kept her face turned
towards him as she made her rounds.

He was more intent on
what was close by.
He was myopic after all
but kept losing his glasses.

Near the end, her presence
went mostly unnoticed.
He retired to his Xanadu
where he had her portrait
set in the ceiling.

Every night he played
the mandolin
and sang love songs
to his painted moon.

LOVE

I see us: survivors
of a house fire where we lost
everything, even our skin.
I practice gestures
with my rebuilt hand
but it slides undetected
over your grafts, nerves
destroyed in the burning.
We flinch from those
who brush past us.
Though we no longer feel,
the fear of touch is real.
Once it erupts, we shrink
into shadow, yearning for what
we may not endure.

## MUSKOKA FALL

Those last years. Before your father died.
Before the stroke stopped your mother's
careless tongue. Before your brother
tore down the paned casements
and cedar-lined rooms. A century lost in a day.
Before he set there something new,
vinyl windows, aluminum siding.

          Before this,
we would head to Lake Rosseau, witness
the silent fire capture the shoreline.
Do you remember the wind?
Waking up chilled under quilts
in the screened-in veranda?
The table scattered with maple leaf stars?
A scarlet corona that set
our daughter's hair aflame?

Tea served up in pink china
out-of-doors with the sky bluer against
its frame of gold and orange.

The end, radiant, around us.

## SCALES

Strange how the space that love once claimed
shrinks.
The fifty-foot kiss on the drive-in movie screen
shrivelled to FaceTime on a mobile phone.

Red cedar to bonsai.
Rainforest to root-bound rubber plant.
Milky Way to a shooting star.

The dance floor tilts beneath our feet
and the ship's wide deck folds
into a solo rower's shell.

## ECHO 3

Some claim the great cow-eyed goddess stole
the nymph's tongue in order to get some work done.
But truly, love, or something like it, silenced her.
From the moment she met that man, she hung
on each word he spoke. She warmed them
like hatching eggs. Or you might say she strung
them together, wore them like a noose
of pearls. She repeated his words to anyone
who would listen. Especially back to him,
so he might turn toward her, if only
to hear himself. Her eyes became mirrors.
She only moved when he did.
Her body faded and left no flower.
Her speech shrank to a whisper of his.
No longer herself, nor him neither.

## ARTERY

She is draining all the colour
from the house, he whispers
to his Blackwood etchings.

He lingers in the living room.
Dust outlines a rectangle
on the blank wall.

On the other side of town
her apartment pulses scarlet.
She straightens a frame.

My blood, she thinks,
catching sight of an ashen face
in the long hall mirror.

## ECHO 4, THERAPY

After she left him at the pond
she was disembodied.

> The counsellor asks,
> *Can you feel your feet?*

They are gone and she is four,
lost in ranks of Campbell soup
and lima beans.

> *What do you miss?*
> A hand whispers
> in the hollow of her back.

She misses the dead, her mother.
Nursing her babies. Drinking coffee
on the weathered steps to the beach
with the house full of sleepers.

> *How does your body feel now?*

She misses tethering the boat,
the hydrostatic pressure at the ocean floor,
rope, chain and anchor, her life that was
sequestered and necessary. The selkies at play,
phosphorescent in dark water.

## ALL IS LOST

In the first dull light, fog slides
between trees on the island
like fingers through hair.
And I, who watched the stars burn
clear through the night and touched
Orion's belt and spear, who saw Mars
aim his red beam across the strait
before he set, who took my bearing
and planned the next brave step,
I burrow into feathers,
drift away in the haze.

# DOG GONE

My dog slipped away yesterday evening
while I sat on the beach and said good-bye
to the man I'd promised a lifetime.
We were catching the last rays
of the August sun.

My dog slipped behind us, vanished
into the long grass of the neighbour's yard.
We searched, but he eluded us.
Later I went to bed, too tired to really care.

Twice I woke to his bark. I called
but he did not come. Sleepless and alone
in the dark, the familiar anger returned.
I listened to the curl and take of the waves,
turned on the bedside light.

Again his bark. I stormed to the deck
and saw the golden shadow on the far lawn.
Slowly he came, reluctant to leave
his freedom, to meet my furious love.

# GRIEF

That was the winter the tide rose
so high the house and cedars
went underwater. The little light left
was green. It was hard to move,
every step a push against sea wash.

When I climbed into the car
to drive to higher ground
the steering wheel was gone,
an octopus in its place.
I couldn't see out
the window for tentacles.

Cedar boughs swung soundlessly.
Sword ferns alone seemed at home.

I don't remember when the tide
turned and withdrew,
only that white rings of barnacles
hold fast to my bathroom wall.

## LOST EARRING

You had them made for me.
My favourite gem. Tsavorite garnet
green as a granny smith.

You lagged a year or so behind my taste.
Go-big-or-go-home had become something
more restrained. When the jeweler changed
the long gold dangle for a small pearl,
they made a perfect pair.

I lost one once at the theatre coat check
but it was found. A little bent
but mendable. Small miracle.
Now it's happened again and this time
it's gone, like you,
and there will be no curtain call.

It could be deep in the crease
of a cab's back seat or stuck
in the loop of a hotel drain,
crushed like a bottle cap in blacktop.

The one that remains is perfect
and perfectly useless.
It hangs beside the mirror
like an accusation.
One-eyed stare. Teardrop pearl.

## TIME

There is no present, no future for her.
There is only a washed-out photograph,
its edges curling on the bulletin board.
Sometimes she hears his laugh, sharp
like a dog's bark. The silence deepens
around the telephone. Old letters drop
unexpectedly out of books.
The mailbox is empty
and what does come is for him and this after
two years. Each morning, she leans against
the window pane, hoping
for something to coax her into the day
but too soon she slides back into the arms
of the unquiet ghost, no longer him,
but her own late self.

## LACHRYMATORY

Tear flasks made in Hebron.
Glass swirled green and blue.
Tiny jars of grief.

When it's full, you're done.
Seal it. Bury.
With the one you lost.

## WHAT IS NECESSARY

It feels like rain this morning.
Something rustles under
the felled Douglas fir.
Crows bark and waves smack the shore,
insistent as a needy child who asks
and asks in a rhythmic mewl until
he loses his longing in singsong.
Across the strait, the island lies
under a band of rose
like a woman in bed,
eyes shut against the rising
clamour of the day.

No one needs her —
the truth hits like the sharp
scent of resin —
no one depends on her.
Busy with cedar posts,
the wasp investigates
then ignores her.
A hummingbird waits
on the hemlock for her
to move aside
from the Spanish broom.

And what, she wonders,
does it matter? She wakes,
sleeps, moves or not as
she will. The hummingbird,
now bold within the stillness,
sips the yellow blooms
and hovers
a wingspan from her face
before it too lifts away.

# BEFORE

What does it mean? She shivers
in her camisole as she rinses
out the pollen's slash across
the breast of white cotton.

She found his profusion of lilies
dying of thirst, rushed them reckless
to the sink to fill the vase with water.
Clip the stems, cull dead blossoms
and rally those still blooming,
those not yet open.

The stain blanches to pale citrine
as she scrubs her blouse,
but a trace remains.

## DOG DAYS

The dog is calm after his all-night summer-time roll.
Who knows where he's been?
Too much time confined is no good for anyone, is it?
Yesterday he broke the grape stake fence and escaped.
Vandalism of the neglected.

It's that kind of desperation that rises up and pushes us
out of tidy lives, compels us past rules and roles' taut noose.
It paddles us out to the small island, to snoop on the shy ones
in hand-built cabins. It pitches us naked into the ocean at midnight,
green stars streaming through webbed fingers.
It steals us behind the back garden to sniff out
the neighbour's scraps, nuzzle lips, all sweat and desire,
to swim in wild grass while Shasta daisies
keep a golden-eyed look out.

## AFTER THE RETREAT

They lie awake until morning
in separate cinderblock rooms.
Outside snow falls
too fast for plows.
But the driver's experienced,
the car well-engineered,
the tires grip.

They leave behind the silence,
drive through mountain blizzard,
hidden ice. Secrets unfold
in the warm interior.
A crease at the back of his neck,
dark hair below knuckles,
his damaged fingernail
stir infinite tenderness.
Both welcome halted traffic
on the highway. Whiteout.

She knows the journey's end.
How his car door will close,
taillights disappear
down the frozen road.
She knows what waits for her,
the frigid house,
the numb embrace,
no power for days.

## ROMANCE

The words on the page lie facedown
on worn cotton until phrases saturate the sheets.

An urgent hand guides her. Breath blows on eyelids,
a gutteral gasp in the crease of her neck.
A threadbare metaphor pulls her hair, tugs
her mouth open and stops
her grunt with its wet fingers.

The book migrates to the empty side,
into the imprint of a nonexistent other.
Tomorrow she'll return it to the library.

Tomorrow she will launder the linen, pull it tight
over the turned mattress. Mitre corners.
Trim and tucked in like her mother taught her.

But for now she lays her cheek in the pillow's dip,
its musk and word-seep. And she weeps.

## SESSION

He grips my hip as I lie curled
on the raised bed. A twist
and then he leaves for others
who wait behind white curtains
in other beds. I nod off, then wake
to hands kneading up and down
my back. He slides under my shirt, past
the waistband of my skirt, lower.
I roll supine and he enfolds me.
His fingers probe then thrust hard
and lift my spine. He holds my pelvis
steady, pushes sideways
with his chest, his breath
on my belly. He comes and goes
and comes again. Wide-awake eyes
close to the delicious nip of pulled hair,
strands caught when he slips fingers
into indents at skull's base, tugs.
He shakes my rib cage side to side,
pats my hair like a favourite pet.
All done. He whispers,
*Let's keep this up. You're coming along.*

## SUBTITLES

The night I left my mother at home
alone to see a movie with a new man,
all the teenage terror came back.
Me, suddenly, ridiculously, single.

I kissed her goodbye while his car
idled in the alley. She brushed aside
her hairpins and I placed tea
in a porcelain cup beside her —
pink glaze smudged across the lines,
the gilt rim worn.

I can't recall what I saw — just
the flickering screen. Him,
silent and foreign. His touch
not forbidden but seeming so.

Later I bent over her bed, touched
her cheek. *You must be freezing,*
she whispered and opened
her eyes, smiled. In a ring of light
outside her window,
the first flakes of snow.

## THE DAY I DROPPED OFF MY WEDDING DRESS
## AT THE SALLY ANN

A prime number
is divisible by itself and one.
You were the one, I thought.

*Twenty-nine*

We were married on that day
and I was that old.
I tried to keep it even,
round it off.

*Thirty going on*
        *forty going on*
                *fifty*

Gathering air miles, houses, dress sizes.
Discarding parts that did not fit:
career, shoulders, a left knee,
principles.

*Fifty-nine*

I enjoy my solitude, though am not unsociable.
Welcome candlelit dinners with friends,
find solace in sisters, am loyal
to the lover who leaves me whole.

HOW THE LIGHT CHANGES

## HOWE SOUND

Dinner is over
but the grey man pours brandy into espresso
so he can stay drunk and awake. Conversation decays
into sentiment. Gets looped.

He remembers
the first time he met you fifty years ago:
a party, a city beach.

You were ready
to let go on a curve of the road to Whistler.
One last fling and you'd fly, hands off the wheel,
sink unseen into the sound's black arm.

But that night
you met, he was so crammed with today
and tomorrow that he had no room for loss.
His eyes widened when you told him your plan
and somehow you were saved.

He doesn't remember
that part, his memory ambered in comfort.
He ingests slow drugs, leaks easy tears. The taxi arrives.
Most times he's wise enough not to drive at night.
His exhaled goodbye wreathes your head in smoke.

Tonight your car's so cold.
You pull away from the old urge, and twist
down the highway. Moon crests the peaks.
Below the sheer drop, water glitters.

## AWAKE

Bathroom tiles stab like ice at 4 a.m. Give up,
get up and get on with the day.
The pulp mill on the other side of the strait throws
lurid yellow on low clouds. False dawn.

She hears a car labour up the hill. People
with somewhere to go. A new generation
leaves for work. To trade hollow bonds and bundles,
to tear up forests and wire the towers,
to steer drones into homes half a world away.

The winter's nighted mornings draw out
dark thoughts like a poultice. The dog sleeps
with one eye open and she is the old woman who
sits by the fire, face half-lit like a lunar eclipse.

# CRASH

Her best painkiller curls
around her shoulders
like a bold exotic
bird, all feathered hair,
green and teal blue.
Slender tattooed fingers
tender escape, smooth
fists whisper

*SAIL AWAY*

but the wound's
heavy metal
is an anchor
weighing
her down.

# CANCER WARD

1

She holds his hand, smooth as wax.
His gold band gleams
as the young man fades.
Already he seems a world away.
Heavy lids make half
circles of bright blue.
Body all edges under a thin gown.
Face sharp as a drawn arrow.

She thinks release —
one high arc
away from here,
from these who crowd
the room with their need,
from the hapless scent
of lilacs and lilies
wilting between machines.
Orchids, the better choice,
those attentive faces,
almost immutable.

She holds his hand
and spans the space between them.
He meets her gaze. Stays.

2

A time is coming when she'll walk   alone through woods
into grey evenings   watch ferns unfurl green fire
in the shadows.   She'll wander
along deer tracks   mossy outcrops   to the water's dark edge
where the otter   shape-shifter   swims toward
the abandoned dock.


3

Outside the building, cumulus
soaks up the day's last light
while high high above
cirrus gather rays
from a fallen sun and slash
a band of gold across the sky.

## PASSAGE

*for Chris*

Day breaks and the island
across the strait
seems so close, seems
to approach.
The human eye can almost
spot tiny houses shining

in the soft morning light.
They seem
overexposed.
Behind them, clouds shadow
the island's spine.

Perhaps death is like this too.
Some days the veil blows away
in a brisk spring breeze
and we see across to the other side.
We look for him there.
Or there, on the passing ferry deck,
gold coins in his eyes,
palm raised in salute.

See how the light changes now,
the cloud shrouds the far shore?
How it fades from our latter-day sight?

# AUBADE

*For Trina*

Only last Christmas she threw away the drugs and it was
all love, love, love until it wasn't. I'd never seen her so happy
and I'd known her since she was one, when we got her
like a puppy my brother picked up and brought home.

Her blue eyes open and she sees me. *Bubala*, she says,
then drifts away. Back then every night, the same book:
*Are You My Mother?* She was an upstart, a pesky
add-on. *Bubala.* I come, sit at the edge of the bed.

She's been lying here for weeks now waiting to die.
The cancer moves from breast to brain like a kid climbing
monkey bars. She's left her little man at home.
She needs to do it alone.

*Look after my Ben. Keep him in the family.* Yes, yes. I will, I will,
I lie to her. I am so shy here, trying to make up lost time. Too late,
too late. I washed her in the kitchen sink, all pink skin, pint-sized.
Those corkscrew curls all gone. *Why should a dog, a horse, a rat
      have life . . .*

November rain strips the trees, washes all meaning
from the skies. I don't deserve the commission. I fought her
so often, failed to protect her. One last chance to let her down.

# THE TOWNHOUSE

Furnished like a sepia photograph.
Quiet despite the river of cars on Kingsway.
It's as if this place holds the imprint
of the two who lived here.
Tenderness wraps the rooms.
Love, drawn out in full before its time,
tints the corners and shadows still.

But the fleshy tulips picked
to brighten the kitchen, they
slash the air, each red petal edged
with yellow, brash as hope.

## RESTLESS

Her mind leaves before her body,
the bulletin board out of tacks.
She drifts down scattered streets.
Newspaper insert tossed
on the breeze. One time
the mailman brings her back
like a lucky guess.

Her Harlequins jam with prompts,
sticky notes declare who did what when
but nothing stops the mind's Osterizer.
Fact and fiction feed the vortex.
Shreds of memory keep
her bedded with a stranger.

The last night in Seven West,
what is left wanders off
the ward. Did she wait for a gap
in surveillance to make
her escape? Her body,
forlorn, still warm to the touch,
forgotten on a hospital cot.

Outside the curtain, complicit
nurses hover, impatient
to remove the remains,
remake the bed. Erase.

## THE COMMITAL

Dead arbutus blooms
like a springtime cherry.
Ghost from another season.
Winter turns loss
into lace.

This is what burial should be —
upright, dazzling and filigreed —
while white stars
of blessing and hope
sift down confetti.

# MINISTERS OF GRACE

## THE PEARL

She undoes the thin shell
buttons on her blouse.
Her baby roots, then sucks.
As her breasts soften
a bead of milk escapes flushed lips.
It traces the cheek's perfect curve.

She falls
into the bottomless gaze,
looks up to see
her own wide woman face, her jaw's
tenderness.

She gasps like a pearl diver
come up for breath. Everything
lusters for days.

## FLICKER

*Knock! Knock! Knock!*
Drumming against
my bedroom wall.
Something alive inside
behind my head. A nest.
White larvae writhing.

*Wake up! Wake!*
Open up the window,
and it swoops away,
flames blazoned
beneath its wings.

## GREEN SEA

Each morning, angels.
Close by I glimpse a wing,
a head, a back. At times
an entire being.
The small tidy head
overshadowed by wings
that beat beat beat
beneath the surface of things.

When I open my eyes
on the other side of prayer
I see them there
close enough to touch
(though I don't for who knows
what might happen then.)
I watch their silent glide and dive,
ringed radiance. Complete.

When I lose sight
of my angels, as I do
as the day passes by,
who is it that hides?

## PRAYER

Unexpected day, cold and grey.
Only the daffodils like fallen shards of sun
glow among ferns.

Wide-eyed at the lawn's edge,
they coax us out of doors.

We come barefoot in wet grass,
hugging ourselves in thin pajamas.

Who has not seen
their green shoots pierce late snow.

I don't have within me what
makes them grow.

## HOME

A wasp planes the stair rail.
It chooses the softer wood
between grain lines,
peels a curl
and flies off.
See where weathered silver
strips away, reveals reddish gold;
how smooth kiln-dried
two by fours become ridged,
textured.

This is how change happens.

A sliver of wood is chewed into paper
and, somewhere, hidden, a nest forms.

# RUFUS

*after Anne-Marie Turza's*
*"Dear God — and when I say God, I mean the God"*

Dear God,
and when I say God, I mean
the God who darts beside me
with flashes of brilliance
and zips off.

I mean this tiny hot head
who comes out of nowhere,
this whirring presence.

I don't have a feeder
because that would be manipulation
and God needs freedom
as much as I do.

God is a brawler
as big as my thumb.

God loves hanging fuchsias,
Spanish broom,
and everything
that blooms.

Dear God, come taste. Show me
your face, calm within
the whirlwind.

## PINE

A pine blocks the shore path,
felled by winter storms.

What looked so substantial
was shallow-rooted.

A thin dish of upraised earth
over rain-washed bedrock.

I see beyond.
The loss improves the view.

That is not to say it was not beautiful.
Its branches once held eagles.

# ARBUTUS

Originally they paddled here
        from the red deserts of Australia
                guided by wind and stars.
                They change shape each time
                you turn your back.
            Limbo dancers,
        belly dancers —
    they bare their skin
every chance they get,
        strip right where they stand.
            Terracotta's their statement,
                green, their neutral,
                    black their accent
                as they age. You'll find them
            flaunting girlish
        figures beside
    the cedar's girth.
They despise everything
        decidedly deciduous.
                Adaptable as all get out,
                they were contortionists —
                    before they ran away
                    from Cirque de Soleil.
                        Something
                    gets in their way
                and they just grow
            around it. They won't
    move inland, though,
    want waterfront —
    at least a cliffside view.
    Consummate riddlers,
they scribble enigmas
        on their leaves, discard
                them in odd seasons.
            Not all that they seem,
        their roots twist around
mysteries their naked
        torsos will never tell.

# PEACHES

## 1

So modest that fuzz buzz on the lips
like the boy's cheeks and chin
the girl's invisible down
so cuddly the fur the curve
shy but alluring pinchable cheeky cheeky
round adorable ass prime booty.
No wonder the young ones trespass
through orchards on hot afternoons
seeking forbidden groves
where the unplucked glow,
where curious fingers press and caress.

## 2

Hand-picked from a roadside stand,
they sit quietly in the passenger seat,
demure in suede suits.
But oh, that fragrance!
No choice but to salivate,
reach, squeeze. Lips part,
tongue nuzzles and sucks.
One sticky hand clings to the wheel
as the car careens down the highway.

## 3

The corrugated stone at the peach's
red centre has a hard-won wisdom.
It knows when to release.
It bleeds only a little.
Discarded on the road's wide shoulder,

the pit is at peace with all transient things.
Mandorla. It dreams of its youth
in the Kunlun mountains,
of sages and the young prince
who bit into soft flesh
and understood desire.

# GRACE

My prayers are awkward.
They don't fit into my bone case,
snug within cerebrum's grey folds.
They seem to arise from outside,
and bump against my forehead
like bumblebees weighted with scent
and gold, dusted from sweet depths
of Spanish broom. They blunder
into the weathered post,
hardly able to clear it,
hardly able to heft the load.

My cortex pauses its dictation
of today's to-do list to notice
the tiny nudge. It recalls
the radio's claim that each
bumblebee is a flying fifty dollar bill.
My life depends on their drone
and buzz, their daily labour.
Bless them.

# PENTECOST

*Excuse me, I'm not asking for money.*
*It's just —*
She doesn't stay to hear the rest.
*I'm late,* she says, darting up the church steps
out of the rain.

High holy day
when the spirit rushed in
and flames licked the apostles' crowns.
A wind blew them into the street
where crowds pointed and called them
drunk.

But the few who lingered,
who listened, understood.

The words spoken. The words not heard.

## WHAT SHE CARRIES

Under the tailored jacket, her waistband bites.
A cell phone vibrates, snug beside her thigh.

At the sea wall, a winter sun ices clouds
pink and gold. A cormorant dips and spears
a spangled fish thick as its gullet, swallows it whole.

The tide is low. All the round stones
are heaped above the ocean's steep edge.
So many round round stones.

# CHICKADEES

*for Sylvia*

When daybreak came,
you walked into the bush
away from the house,
while your children
slept in the attic room.

Your nightdress dragged
like a bridal train
collecting burrs.

You climbed
into the maple's crook.
Nine came then, fluttering.

How they caressed the sorrowing air,
those winged and feathered ministers.

# GLENELG, SOUTH AUSTRALIA

When next the breeze
lures you to the blue pier
(carrying you where people fish,
men and boys with long poles,
girls who put down crab traps
and eat their lunch
squatting on the cement),
take time to stand
under the Aeolian harp.

Taut silver wires deliver
chord and discord with every gust.
This is the sound of what lifts
the seagulls' wings,
what leads the great dance
of wave and cloud.

Does the wind pluck
your sorrow? Clutch at your plans?
Can you stay till your heart yields
to that wilder strain?

Then, come back to the shore.
Sing to the emptiness.

# REPRISE

I always thought I might meet her again
in a small brown sparrow.
So you can imagine my shock
when there she was.
All peacock. Feather and fan.
No peahen in sight.
Its call reminded me
she never could sing.

Male?
Maybe not such a surprise.
It was my father who made her
weak-kneed, doe-eyed
and pregnant, constantly.
She ordered the doctor
to tie her tubes when they removed
half her ulcered stomach.
At least that's how I heard it.

Peacock? Show off?
There was that time she jumped
on the table and danced
with the jingling bellydance man.
Yes.
She loved her fine figure.
When we were poor, she sewed
satin dresses from rummage sale finds,
flounced blouses from frayed shirts.

Toward the end she lost her memory
but not her vanity.
She strutted into Bible Study
flaunting shapely legs among the infirm.
Peacock.
Tactless, sometimes,
breathtaking.

# HYDROGENY

Stars drip honey into night sea.
Fish shoot meteor showers.
Slip into black water,
light quake.
Sparkles sidle between fingers,
slither over wrists.

Once upon a time on a night like this,
I shook daughters from drowsy beds.
Pajamas dropped on pebbles
and we glided like starspray,
flew through galaxies of startled water.

Tonight, alone,
concentric circles of iced fire
wave out bright rings.
A green firework explodes below —
seal, whale, rising city of light?

## AT HOME

So much is left undone.
Burdock grows rank around the steps.
Hops climb in the windows
like corkscrew assassins,
clothed in innocent green.
The transparent apple tree scrapes the roof
and the lilacs' suckers rub the siding,
bridges for carpenter ants.

A poet shouldn't live in a house.
The weight of what is neglected,
those hefty timbers, unpeopled stories,
might crush her hummingbird words.

## BUMBLEBEE

I thought it was
my lover's fingers
tapping
on the high window
above the bed.
I opened my eyes
and found my hair
tangled with jasmine
and leaf shadows
whispering
from the bright walls.

## LIBATION

The pool beside the path brims again.
Stones shine through depths.
Ferns arch across the mirror.

It was not always so.
Remember when summer claimed
every drop of rain for weeks
turned years. Remember when
sodden tangles of leaves,
and once, a fallen tree,
diverted the course,
left the basin empty.

Now in midwinter,
the stream spills in
and out over the lip,
away through bracken.

The pool swells and stays
perfectly still.

# MOON OVER MATHEWS RANGE, KENYA

The bush pilot unbuttons his shirt to show us
the cicatrice, a small moon, on his sternum.
All that is left of a bullet to the chest, unless you count
the hate that shimmers through him, overflows the rim
of his glass, fan dances in the campfire.

Camels *nuzz, nuzz,* desert muezzins. Once in awhile,
the cough of a lion. In the distance, men sing
in parched river beds as they have, I think, forever.
Time widens these plains. Memory palpable
as that nub of thickened skin, as red earth.

Eva says something is eating the moon and we all look up,
watch it turn blood orange. Eclipse.
I tuck the mosquito net under my daughters' mattress.
They slap each other, then laugh. The young are like cheetahs.
They bolt the soft belly of their prey and then sleep.

O in this life bless us with the camel's foot and eye.
May we walk over the shifting surface of things
and not sink. The long lashes and that clear inner eyelid
to protect our sight yet let in light to see.

# HINDSIGHT

She's crying in the girl's can,
the last stall by the window.
She slides back the latch to leave
but the sobs catch, and she sags
onto the toilet's black rim.
She pulls up slumping knee socks.
In her rush to get out of the house,
she left the red elastics she likes to tuck
under the white ribbing. She touches
the bump at the back of her head.
She'd been shouting through the house,
looking for socks when he slammed her
against the fridge. Her head ricocheted back
and caught the freezer handle.

I go to her through the door
*Wish he were dead*, she says and presses
her hard breast buds into me.
I whisper that she's a good girl,
that fathers have no right to hurt
their daughters. I remind her
he's been drinking more since
his younger brother died last month.
I stroke her hair and let her tuck
her arms tight under mine.
I don't say that he does love her
even though he doesn't show it anymore.
I don't say she too has his short fuse.

## ADVENT

Angels everywhere.

*Hide me under the shadow of your wings.*

The ships have brought their gifts
from east to west.
Cold feet stuffed in wool socks
venture into the port city's glow,
this world's dying sun.

*In the shadow of wings.*

What tidings from on high?
A request? A whispered promise?
Gloria or the fiery sword?

*In the shadow.*

The gifts lie discarded, tarnished.
Take them back.
Change or exchange.
May love have a second coming.

*Hide me under the shadow of your wings.*

# WHEN

When I become the sea,
I will touch every shore at the same time.
I will pull up foamy skirts and show off my purple stars.
I will swell, crest and fume,
     send salt spray sideways
     etch the beach house windows.
I will rage.
I will hurl tree trunks, twist aluminum boats
     and bury them under rock.
I will soothe.
I will cradle the moon and trace her river of light,
     when I become the sea.